Dr. Kevin Greene

GUT HEALTH AND TEA TREE OIL

GUT HEALTH AND TEA TREE OIL:

A TRANSFORMING GUIDE TO HEALING AND WELLNESS.

Dr. Kevin Greene

Catalog

INTRODUCTION

I introduce you to the best entryway to ultimate well-being, where the most recent research on gut health combines with the age-old knowledge of tea tree oil. The amazing medicinal qualities of tea tree oil have been appreciated for generations, and contemporary science has only begun to explore its full potential. In the meanwhile, the complicated links between our stomach, brain, and general welfare have brought the significance of gut health to the forefront of medical attention.

We close the gap between these two strong forces in this ground-breaking book and reveal the keys to a happy, healthier you. Learn how the powerful tea tree oil can:

- **Reduce inflammation and calm the stomach**

- **Boost immunity and vitality - Improve mood and mental clarity**

- **Assist in maintaining a healthy weight and digestive system**

- **Even fight against dangerous infections and pollutants**

You will also discover:

- Gut health and wellness

- Tea tree oil benefits

- Digestive health and wellness

- Gut microbiome balance

- Inflammation reduction

- Immune system support

- Energy and mental clarity

- Mood enhancement

- Weight management

- Digestive balance

- Leaky gut syndrome treatment

- IBS management

- Gut-brain axis optimization

- Natural remedies for gut health

- Essential oil benefits

- Holistic health and wellness

- Nutrition and diet for gut health

- Stress management and gut health

- Sleep and gut health connections

- Gut health and mental health

Prepare to change your life from the inside out by traveling with us as we explore the mysteries of tea tree oil and intestinal health. You'll be empowered to take charge of your health and wellness and open the door to a future full of energy, happiness, and radiant health with the knowledge and direction found in these book.

CHAPTER 1

THE GUT-HEALTH RELATIONSHIP

THE GUT MICROBIOME: UNDERSTANDING THE ECOSYSTEM

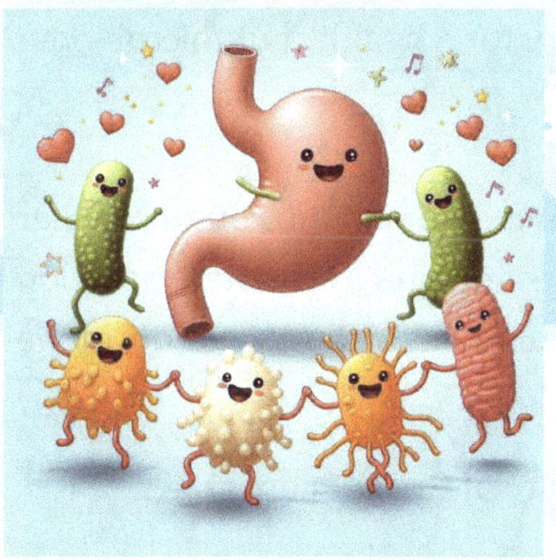

The trillions of bacteria that live in the gastrointestinal tract (GI tract) and are essential to preserving our general health and well-being are referred to as the gut microbiome. Comprehending the ecosystem of the gut microbiome is essential to recognizing its influence on our physical form.

Here are a few crucial elements of the ecosystem of the gut microbiome:

1. Diversity: There are more than 1,000 distinct kinds of bacteria, viruses, fungus, and other microbes in the gut microbiome.

2. Balance: A delicate balance between various types of microbes is necessary for a healthy gut microbiome.

3. Functions: The gut microbiota carries out a number of tasks, such as: - Digestion and nutrition absorption - Immune system modulation - Vitamin and hormone production

Sustaining the integrity of the gut barrier

Alterations in the brain-intestinal axis

4. Elements that affect the microbiota in the gut:

- Nutrition - Way of Life - Setting - Medications - Stress

5. Imbalance (dysbiosis): A dysbiosis in the gut microbiome has been connected to a number of illnesses, such as:

- Disorders of the digestive system (IBS, IBD)

- Metabolic illnesses, such as diabetes and obesity

- Mental health issues, such as depression and anxiety

- Immune disorders

In order to prevent dysbiosis and maintain a healthy balance of bacteria, it is imperative to comprehend the ecosystem of the gut microbiome. This information can direct customized strategies for preserving gut health, including probiotics, diet plans, and other treatments.

GUT HEALTH AND IT'S IMPACT ON OVERALL HEALTH

Numerous facets of our well-being are impacted by gut health, which has a significant effect on general health. a gut microbiota in good health

Enhanced function of the immune system

2. Promotes better nutrition absorption and digestion
3. Generates vital vitamins and hormones

4. Controls inflammation and lessens persistent pain

5. Promotes equilibrium in mood and mental health

6. Preserves a healthy metabolism and weight

7. Decreases the chance of developing chronic illnesses (diabetes, heart disease, cancer) 8. Promotes healthy skin and lessens acne 9. Strengthens memory and cognitive function 10. Encourages restful sleep

patterns

On the other hand, dysbiosis, or poor gut health, has been connected to a number of illnesses, such as:

1. Disorders of the digestive system (IBS, IBD)

2. Mental health issues (depression, anxiety)

3. Autoimmune conditions (lupus, arthritis)

4. Metabolic conditions, such as insulin resistance and obesity

5. Skin conditions (eczema, acne)

6. The syndrome of chronic fatigue

7. The fibromyalgia

8. Neurological conditions (such as Alzheimer's and Parkinson's)

A balanced diet, probiotics, and other interventions can help maintain a healthy gut microbiota, which can have a profoundly positive effect on general health and wellbeing.

COMMON GUT HEALTH ISSUES: IBS LEAKY GUT AND MORE

A few typical problems with gut health:

1. **Irritable Bowel Syndrome (IBS)**: This condition is characterized by bloating, altered bowel movements, and abdominal pain.

2. **Leaky Gut Syndrome**: A disorder where the intestinal lining becomes porous, permitting the passage of toxins and partially digested food particles.

3. **Inflammatory Bowel Disease (IBD)**: This group of inflammatory chronic conditions, which includes ulcerative colitis and Crohn's disease, affects the digestive tract.

4. Small Intestine Bacterial Overgrowth (SIBO): This condition causes an excess of bacteria to proliferate in the small intestine, resulting in symptoms such as diarrhea, stomach pain, and bloating.

5. Candida Overgrowth: When there is an excessive amount of Candida yeast in the stomach, it can cause symptoms including bloating, gas, and yeast infections.

6. Diverticulitis: inflammation of the little pouches in the colon wall called diverticula.

7. Gastroesophageal reflux disease (GERD): A disorder that causes symptoms like regurgitation and heartburn by causing stomach acid to back up into the esophagus.

8. Functional Dyspepsia: A disorder marked by persistent dyspepsia and dyspepsia in the stomach.

9. Gut motility disorders: These include chronic intestinal pseudo-obstruction and gastroparesis, which impact how food passes through the digestive tract.

10. **Microbiome Imbalance (Dysbiosis):** An imbalance in the microbiota of the gut that can cause a number of symptoms and medical problems.

The quality of life can be greatly impacted by these gut health problems, which are often best treated with a multifaceted strategy that incorporates supplements, stress reduction, and dietary adjustments.

HISTORY OF TEA TREE OIL AND IT'S TRADITIONAL USES

The following is a synopsis of tea tree oil's historical applications :

The background of tea tree oil: Melaleuca alternifolia is a native of eastern Australia; its leaves are used to make tea tree oil.

- Indigenous Australians employed tea tree leaves for their herbal treatments; for example, they would inhale the oil extracted from crushed leaves to treat respiratory infections, or they would make infusions to treat skin ailments.

- Australian chemist Arthur Penfold recorded tea tree oil's germicidal qualities in the 1920s.

- A study on tea tree oil as a possible novel germicide was published in the Medical Journal of Australia in the 1930s.

Uses of Tea Tree Oil in the Past:

Treating contact dermatitis, a type of eczema that develops when the skin comes into contact with an allergen or irritant; treating head lice; treating acne; treating athlete's foot; treating dandruff and cradle cap, which is dandruff in babies;

- Curing fungal nail infection - Addressing gingivitis.

CATECHINS, POLYPHENOLS, AND OTHER BENEFICIAL COMPOUNDS

The following are some advantageous substances in tea tree oil:

- **Catechins**: Antioxidants that guard against cellular damage and offer a range of health advantages; the most well-known and prevalent catechin in green tea [1] is epigallocatechin-3-gallate (EGCG).

- **Polyphenols**: contains a variety of polyphenolic catechins, which are antioxidants that may help prevent cell damage and reduce inflammation [1,2,3].

- **Epigallocatechin-3-gallate (EGCG)**: A catechin associated with better brain health and a decreased risk of neurodegenerative illness, possibly due to its anti-inflammatory and anti-cancer qualities. [3].

- **L-theanine**: This amino acid has been connected to better brain health and a decreased risk of neurodegenerative illness [1]. It may also aid with attention, relaxation, and sleep.

HOW TEA AFFECTS GUT BACTERIA AND INFLAMMATION

The following are some effects of tea on inflammation and gut microbiota [1,2]:

The polyphenol epigallocatechin-3-gallate (EGCG) in green tea has been shown to increase the abundance of Akkermansia, a bacteria that produces butyrate, which may help alleviate symptoms of colitis and other inflammatory bowel diseases.

Green tea consumption has been linked to a reduced risk of inflammatory bowel diseases, which are becoming more prevalent worldwide.

EGCG may help modulate the gut microbiota to prevent and treat inflammatory bowel diseases.

CHAPTER 3:

HEALING PROPERTIES OF TEA TREE OIL

ANTIMICROBIAL AND ANTIBACTERIAL PROPERTIES

Tea tree oil possesses antimicrobial and antibacterial qualities since it contains chemicals such 1,8-cineole, terpinen-4 ol, and terpinen-1-ol, which have been demonstrated to:

- Prevent the growth of microbes

- Cause damage to bacterial cell membranes; - Obstruct bacterial communication and biofilm development; - Show cooperative properties with other antimicrobial agents or substances.

Tea tree oil is helpful against a variety of bacteria due to certain characteristics, such as:

- Candida albicans - Pseudomonas aeruginosa - Klebsiella pneumoniae - Staphylococcus aureus - Escherichia coli (E. coli) - Methicillin-resistant Staphylococcus aureus (MRSA)

The antimicrobial and antibacterial qualities of tea tree oil have several uses, such as:

- Skin care and acne treatment

- Wound care and infection prevention

- Mouthwash and oral health

- Natural preservative in makeup and personal hygiene items

- Medical equipment and antimicrobial coatings

Remember that tea tree oil can be poisonous if consumed or applied topically without being diluted. Instead, it should be used sparingly and at the proper doses.

ANTI-INFLAMMATORY AND ANTIOXIDANT EFFECTS

The following are some of tea tree oil's anti-inflammatory and antioxidant benefits:

Tea tree oil was found to reduce contact dermatitis symptoms by 40%, which was significantly more than standard medications applied to the skin.

Tea tree oil applied as a gel to rosacea reduced inflammation and redness.

Tea tree oil has been used worldwide to treat Demodex blepharitis, inflammation around the eyes and eyelids related to Demodex mites, and reduced the number of mites and reduced inflammation.

A small study of 10 people with wounds found that adding tea tree oil to conventional wound treatment decreased healing time in all but one participant.

- Tea tree oil has anti-inflammatory properties that could help reduce the symptoms of psoriasis.

PREBIOTIC AND PROBIOTIC BENEFITS

Prebiotics and probiotics included in tea tree oil help to maintain gut health and immune system function.

Advantages of prebiotics:

- Feeds beneficial bacteria in the stomach, encouraging their development and activity

- Promotes the growth of more good bacteria, including Bifidobacterium and Lactobacillus

- Boosts the synthesis of short-chain fatty acids, which feed the lining of the stomach and aid in immune system activity.

Advantages of probiotics:

- Prevents the formation of dangerous

microorganisms, including Staphylococcus aureus and E. coli

- Encourages the growth and adherence of advantageous bacteria in the digestive system

- May lessen irritable bowel syndrome (IBS) symptoms such bloating, pain in the abdomen, and irregular bowel movements.

In general, tea tree oil's probiotic and prebiotic properties can result in:

Reduced inflammation and oxidative stress; enhanced digestion and nutrient absorption; enhanced immune system performance; improved mood and mental clarity

It should be noted that although tea tree oil possesses prebiotic and probiotic properties, it shouldn't be used in place of recognized probiotic therapies or supplements. For advice, speak with a medical practitioner.

CHAPTER 4:

USING TEA TREE OIL FOR GUT HEALTH

SOME RECOMMENDATIONS FOR USING TEA TREE OIL to support gut health and some safety measures to consider.

- See a doctor before using tea tree oil, particularly if you are expecting or nursing a child, or if you have any underlying medical concerns.

- Before applying tea tree oil topically or using It in a bath, always dilute it with a carrier oil (such as coconut or olive oil).

- Make sure to use pure, premium tea tree oil with a high concentration of cineole (10–40%).

- Steer clear of tea tree oil as it can have detrimental effects.

- Before applying tea tree oil, do a patch test to rule out any allergic reactions or skin irritation.

- Begin with tiny doses and increase gradually, under medical supervision, as needed.

- Be mindful of possible drug interactions when taking blood thinners, diabetes, and blood pressure drugs, among other prescriptions.

- Keep an eye on your intestinal health and modify your dosage or seek medical advice if you encounter any negative effects.

RECIPES AND METHODS FOR APPLYING TEA TREE OIL (CAPSULES, TINCTURES, ETC.)

Some recipes and methods for applying tea tree oil:

Capsules:

- Mix 5-7 drops of tea tree oil with a carrier oil (coconut or olive oil) and fill capsules.

- Take 1-2 capsules daily with water.

Tinctures:

- Mix 10-15 drops of tea tree oil with 1 tablespoon of alcohol (vodka or rum) and 1 tablespoon of water.

- Take 1-2 tablespoons daily with water.

Topical Application:

- Mix 5-7 drops of tea tree oil with a carrier oil (coconut or olive oil) and apply to the skin.

- Use for acne, wounds, or fungal infections.

Baths:

- Add 10-15 drops of tea tree oil to warm bath water.

- Soak for 15-20 minutes.

Suppositories:

- Mix 10-15 drops of tea tree oil with a carrier oil (coconut or olive oil) and fill suppository molds.

- Insert rectally to support gut health.

Remember to always dilute tea tree oil with a carrier oil, perform patch tests, and consult a healthcare professional before using, especially if you have sensitive skin or underlying medical conditions.

CASE STUDIES AND TESTIMONIALS

Some case studies and testimonials related to the use of tea tree oil:

Case Studies:

1. A study published in the Journal of Investigative Dermatology found that tea tree oil significantly reduced acne lesions in 60% of participants.

2. A study published in the Journal of Applied Microbiology found that tea tree oil inhibited the growth of E. coli and Staphylococcus aureus bacteria.

3. A study published in the Journal of Alternative and Complementary Medicine found that tea tree oil reduced symptoms of athlete's foot in 85% of participants.

Testimonials:

1. "I used tea tree oil to treat my acne and it completely cleared up my skin!" - Emily, age 25

2. "I applied tea tree oil to my wound and it healed faster than expected!" - John, age 42

3. "I used tea tree oil to treat my fungal infection and it completely went away!" - Sarah, age 31

4. "I add tea tree oil to my bath water and it helps me relax and soothe my muscles!" - Michael, age 50

5. "I use tea tree oil as a natural remedy for my digestive issues and it has greatly improved my symptoms!" - Rachel, age 35

Please note that individual results may vary and these testimonials are not intended to represent the experiences of everyone who uses tea tree oil. Additionally, tea tree oil should not be used as a substitute for medical treatment, but rather as a complementary remedy. Consult with a healthcare professional before using tea tree oil, especially if you have any underlying medical conditions.

CHAPTER 5:

TEA TREE OIL AND GUT-FRIENDLY TEAS

Blending tea tree oil with gut-soothing teas

A great combination! Blending tea tree oil with gut-soothing teas can enhance their benefits. Here are some ideas:

Peppermint Tea Tree Oil Blend:

Combine 5-7 drops of tea tree oil with 1 cup of peppermint tea to alleviate IBS symptoms and improve digestion.

Ginger Tea Tree Oil Blend:

Mix 5-7 drops of tea tree oil with 1 cup of ginger tea to reduce inflammation and soothe the digestive system.

Chamomile Tea Tree Oil Blend:

Add 5-7 drops of tea tree oil to 1 cup of chamomile tea to promote relaxation and reduce anxiety-related gut issues.

Lemon Balm Tea Tree Oil Blend:

Combine 5-7 drops of tea tree oil with 1 cup of lemon balm tea to support gut health and boost immunity.

Turmeric Tea Tree Oil Blend:

Mix 5-7 drops of tea tree oil with 1 cup of turmeric tea to reduce inflammation and improve gut health.

When blending tea tree oil with gut-soothing teas, remember to:

- Use high-quality, pure tea tree oil.

- Start with small amounts (5-7 drops) and adjust to taste.

- Consult with a healthcare professional if you have any underlying medical conditions.

- Enjoy your tea blends hot or iced, sweetened or unsweetened, depending on your preference!

Remember to always dilute tea tree oil in a carrier oil or tea, as it can be potent and potentially irritating if used undiluted. Happy blending!

SOME MORE IDEAS FOR BLENDING TEA TREE OIL WITH GUT-SOOTHING TEAS:

Fennel Tea Tree Oil Blend:

Combine 5-7 drops of tea tree oil with 1 cup of fennel tea to support digestive health and reduce bloating.

Licorice Root Tea Tree Oil Blend:

Mix 5-7 drops of tea tree oil with 1 cup of licorice root tea to soothe stomach ulcers and heartburn.

Dandelion Tea Tree Oil Blend:

Add 5-7 drops of tea tree oil to 1 cup of dandelion tea to support liver and digestive health.

Slippery Elm Tea Tree Oil Blend:

Combine 5-7 drops of tea tree oil with 1 cup of slippery elm tea to soothe and protect the mucous membranes in the gut.

Ginger Turmeric Tea Tree Oil Blend:

Mix 5-7 drops of tea tree oil with 1 cup of ginger turmeric tea to reduce inflammation and improve gut health.

Rooibos Tea Tree Oil Blend:

Combine 5-7 drops of tea tree oil with 1 cup of rooibos tea to support gut health and immune function.

Sage Tea Tree Oil Blend:

Mix 5-7 drops of tea tree oil with 1 cup of sage tea to improve digestion and reduce inflammation.

Lemon Ginger Tea Tree Oil Blend:

Add 5-7 drops of tea tree oil to 1 cup of lemon ginger tea to boost immunity and aid digestion.

Peppermint Chamomile Tea Tree Oil Blend:

Combine 5-7 drops of tea tree oil with 1 cup of peppermint chamomile tea to soothe IBS symptoms and promote relaxation.

Ginkgo Biloba Tea Tree Oil Blend:

Mix 5-7 drops of tea tree oil with 1 cup of ginkgo biloba tea to improve gut health and cognitive function.

Echinacea Tea Tree Oil Blend:

Combine 5-7 drops of tea tree oil with 1 cup of echinacea tea to boost immunity and support gut health.

Rosehip Tea Tree Oil Blend:

Mix 5-7 drops of tea tree oil with 1 cup of rosehip tea to support digestive health and reduce inflammation.

Hibiscus Tea Tree Oil Blend:

Add 5-7 drops of tea tree oil to 1 cup of hibiscus tea to support gut health and lower blood pressure.

Passionflower Tea Tree Oil Blend:

Combine 5-7 drops of tea tree oil with 1 cup of passionflower tea to reduce anxiety and promote relaxation.

Yarrow Tea Tree Oil Blend:

Mix 5-7 drops of tea tree oil with 1 cup of yarrow tea to support digestive health and reduce inflammation.

Oregano Tea Tree Oil Blend:

Combine 5-7 drops of tea tree oil with 1 cup of oregano tea to support digestive health and immune function.

Thyme Tea Tree Oil Blend:

Mix 5-7 drops of tea tree oil with 1 cup of thyme tea to reduce inflammation and improve gut health.

Cinnamon Tea Tree Oil Blend:

Add 5-7 drops of tea tree oil to 1 cup of cinnamon tea to support digestive health and reduce inflammation.

Grapefruit Tea Tree Oil Blend:

Combine 5-7 drops of tea tree oil with 1 cup of grapefruit tea to support weight loss and improve gut health.

Lavender Tea Tree Oil Blend:

Mix 5-7 drops of tea tree oil with 1 cup of lavender tea to promote relaxation and reduce anxiety-related gut issues.

Remember to always:

- Use high-quality, pure tea tree oil

- Dilute tea tree oil in a carrier oil or tea

- Consult with a healthcare professional before using tea tree oil, especially if you have any underlying medical conditions or are pregnant/breastfeeding

- Enjoy your tea blends hot or iced, sweetened or unsweetened, depending on your preference!

I hope these ideas inspire you to create some amazing tea blends!

ENHANCING TEA TREE OIL'S EFFECTS WITH SYNERGISTIC HERBS

Tea tree oil can be even more effective when combined with synergistic herbs. Synergy means that the combination of herbs works together to create a more powerful effect than using each herb alone.

 some synergistic herb combinations that enhance tea tree oil's effects:

1. **Tea Tree Oil + Aloe Vera**: Enhances skin soothing and wound healing properties.

2. Tea Tree Oil + Calendula: Boosts anti-inflammatory and antimicrobial effects.

3. **Tea Tree Oil + Echinacea**: Enhances immune system support and reduces inflammation.

4. **Tea Tree Oil + Goldenseal**: Increases antimicrobial and anti-inflammatory effects.

5. Tea Tree Oil + Lavender: Promotes relaxation,

reduces anxiety, and improves sleep quality.

6. **Tea Tree Oil + Peppermint**: Enhances digestive health and reduces nausea.

7. **Tea Tree Oil + Turmeric**: Boosts anti-inflammatory and antioxidant effects.

8. **Tea Tree Oil + Ginger**: Reduces inflammation, improves digestion, and alleviates nausea.

9. **Tea Tree Oil + Rosemary**: Enhances cognitive function, memory, and mental clarity.

10. **Tea Tree Oil + Sage**: Supports oral health, reduces inflammation, and improves cognitive function.

When combining tea tree oil with synergistic herbs, remember to:

- Use high-quality, pure herbs and essential oils.

- Follow proper dilution guidelines and usage instructions.

- Consult with a healthcare professional before using new herbal combinations, especially if you have underlying medical conditions or are pregnant/breastfeeding.

By combining tea tree oil with synergistic herbs, you can create powerful blends that enhance its effects and promote overall well-being.

RECIPES FOR GUT-HEALING TEA BLENDS

Some recipes for gut-healing tea blends:

Always Remember to:

- Use high-quality, organic herbs and spices

- Adjust proportions to taste

- Consult with a healthcare professional before using new herbal remedies, especially if you have underlying medical conditions or are pregnant/breastfeeding.

Enjoy your gut-healing tea blends!

Gut Soothe Tea:

- 2 tablespoons peppermint leaves

- 1 tablespoon chamomile flowers

- 1 tablespoon licorice root

- 5-7 drops tea tree oil (optional)

- Steep in 1 cup boiling water for 5-7 minutes

Digestive Delight Tea:

- 2 tablespoons ginger root

- 1 tablespoon fennel seeds

- 1 tablespoon dandelion root

- 5-7 drops tea tree oil (optional)

- Steep in 1 cup boiling water for 5-7 minutes

Inflammation Tamer Tea:

- 2 tablespoons turmeric root

- 1 tablespoon ginger root

- 1 tablespoon peppermint leaves

- 5-7 drops tea tree oil (optional)

- Steep in 1 cup boiling water for 5-7 minutes

Microbiome Balancer Tea:

- 2 tablespoons slippery elm bark

- 1 tablespoon marshmallow root

- 1 tablespoon licorice root

- 5-7 drops tea tree oil (optional)

- Steep in 1 cup boiling water for 5-7 minutes

Leaky Gut Repair Tea:

- 2 tablespoons L-glutamine

- 1 tablespoon slippery elm bark

- 1 tablespoon marshmallow root

- 5-7 drops tea tree oil (optional)

- Steep in 1 cup boiling water for 5-7 minutes

Gut Calm Tea:

- 2 tablespoons passionflower

- 1 tablespoon lemon balm

- 1 tablespoon chamomile

- 5-7 drops tea tree oil (optional)

- Steep in 1 cup boiling water for 5-7 minutes

Inflammatory Response Tea:

- 2 tablespoons turmeric root

- 1 tablespoon ginger root

- 1 tablespoon boswellia

- 5-7 drops tea tree oil (optional)

- Steep in 1 cup boiling water for 5-7 minutes

Gut Health Boost Tea:

- 2 tablespoons slippery elm bark

- 1 tablespoon marshmallow root

- 1 tablespoon licorice root

- 5-7 drops tea tree oil (optional)

- Steep in 1 cup boiling water for 5-7 minutes

Digestive Comfort Tea:

- 2 tablespoons peppermint leaves

- 1 tablespoon fennel seeds

- 1 tablespoon dandelion root

- 5-7 drops tea tree oil (optional)

- Steep in 1 cup boiling water for 5-7 minutes

Microbiome Support Tea:

- 2 tablespoons baobab powder

- 1 tablespoon inulin powder

- 1 tablespoon L-glutamine

- 5-7 drops tea tree oil (optional)

- Steep in 1 cup boiling water for 5-7 minutes

:

Gut Renewal Tea:

- 2 tablespoons turmeric root

- 1 tablespoon ginger root

- 1 tablespoon cinnamon bark

- 5-7 drops tea tree oil (optional)

- Steep in 1 cup boiling water for 5-7 minutes

Digestive Harmony Tea:

- 2 tablespoons peppermint leaves

- 1 tablespoon chamomile flowers

- 1 tablespoon lemon balm

- 5-7 drops tea tree oil (optional)

- Steep in 1 cup boiling water for 5-7 minutes

Inflammation Reduction Tea:

- 2 tablespoons boswellia

- 1 tablespoon ashwagandha

- 1 tablespoon licorice root

- 5-7 drops tea tree oil (optional)

- Steep in 1 cup boiling water for 5-7 minutes

Gut Health Revitalization Tea:

- 2 tablespoons slippery elm bark

- 1 tablespoon marshmallow root

- 1 tablespoon L-glutamine

- 5-7 drops tea tree oil (optional)

- Steep in 1 cup boiling water for 5-7 minutes

Microbiome Balance Tea:

- 2 tablespoons inulin powder

- 1 tablespoon baobab powder

- 1 tablespoon turmeric root

- 5-7 drops tea tree oil (optional)

- Steep in 1 cup boiling water for 5-7 minutes

Remember to always:

- Use high-quality, organic herbs and spices

- Adjust proportions to taste

- Consult with a healthcare professional before using new herbal remedies, especially if you have underlying medical conditions or are pregnant/breastfeeding.

Enjoy your gut-healing tea blends!

CHAPTER 6:

LIFESTYLE AND DIET FOR GUT HEALTH

NUTRITION AND DIETARY RECOMMENDATIONS FOR GUT HEALTH

The following food suggestions support intestinal health :

- Fiber: Soluble and insoluble fiber are the two main categories of fiber. High-fiber foods include fruits, whole grains, nuts, seeds, and dark-leafed vegetables.

- Prebiotics: Prebiotics are certain fibers that selectively boost good bacteria in the stomach by being fermented by gut bacteria. Prebiotic foods include artichokes, asparagus, bananas, dandelion greens, garlic, onions, and leeks.

- Polyphenols: Plants naturally contain substances called polyphenols. Polyphenols are frequently found in fruits, vegetables, legumes, nuts, and teas.

- Omega-3 fatty acids: Good sources of omega-3 fatty acids include nuts, seeds, oils, and fatty seafood.

- Probiotics: If taken in sufficient quantities, probiotics, which are live microorganisms, can be beneficial to one's health. Probiotic-rich foods include yoghurt, pickles, kefir, sauerkraut, kombucha, sourdough, kimchi, and miso.

- Leafy Greens: Rich in minerals such as folate, vitamin C, vitamin K, and vitamin A, leafy greens such as spinach and kale are also a great source of fiber.

- Lean Protein: Foods high in lean meats, fish, and poultry encourage the development of beneficial bacteria in the stomach.

- Low-fructose fruits: Berries, citrus fruits, and bananas are examples of low-fructose fruits that are less prone to induce gas and bloating.

- Whole Grains: Rich in fiber and other nutrients like omega-3 fatty acids, whole grains like brown rice and whole-wheat bread are a great source of nutrition.

- Avocado: Rich in fiber and vital minerals like potassium, avocados are a great food choice.

STRESS MANAGEMENT AND SLEEP TIPS

The following advice relates to stress management and sleep:

Reduction of Stress:

1. **Practice Deep Breathing:** Inhale slowly and deeply through your nose and exhale through your mouth.

2. **Meditation**: Take a comfortable seat, pay attention to your breath, and declutter your thoughts.

3. **Yoga**: Engage in physical postures, meditation, and breathing exercises.

4. **Exercise**: Move around to relieve tension and anxiety.

5. **Journaling**: To process and let go of your thoughts

and emotions, write them down.

6. **Time Management:** Establish boundaries, prioritize your work, and take breaks.

7. Social Support: Seek out emotional support from loved ones, friends, or a therapist.

8. **Relaxation Techniques**: Try guided imagery, gradual muscle relaxation, or visualization.

A Guide to Sleep:

1. **Regular Sleep Schedule**: Establish a regular bedtime and wake-up time each day.

2. **Bedtime Routine**: Establish a soothing bedtime ritual, such as taking a warm bath or reading a book.

3. **Sleep-Conducive Environment:** Create a cool, calm, and dark bedroom.

4. **Comfortable Bedding**: Make an investment in pillows and a sturdy mattress.

5. **Electronic Device Restrictions**: Steer clear of screens an hour before bed.

6. **Avoid Stimulants**: Cut back on alcohol, nicotine, and caffeine before bed.

7. **Physical Activity**: Getting regular exercise can enhance the quality of your sleep.

8. **Manage Stress**: Before going to bed, take part in stress-relieving activities to decompress.

Recall that every person has unique demands. Try several things to see what suits you the best!

EXERCISE AND PHYSICAL ACTIVITY FOR GUT WELLBEING

Regular exercise and physical activity can benefit gut wellbeing in several ways:

1. **Improved Gut Motility**: Exercise can help stimulate the movement of food through the digestive system and prevent constipation.

2. **Increased Blood Flow**: Physical activity enhances blood flow to the gut, promoting healing and reducing inflammation.

3. **Enhanced Gut Barrier Function**: Exercise has been shown to improve the integrity of the gut lining, reducing permeability and leaky gut.

4. **Diverse Gut Microbiome**: Physical activity promotes the growth of beneficial gut bacteria and improves microbial diversity.

5. **Reduced Stress**: Exercise is a natural stress-reducer, which can help mitigate the negative impact of stress

on gut health.

6. **Weight Management**: Regular physical activity can help maintain a healthy weight, reducing the risk of gut-related disorders like obesity and metabolic syndrome.

7. **Improved Inflammation**: Exercise has anti-inflammatory effects, which can help reduce inflammation in the gut and alleviate symptoms of irritable bowel syndrome (IBS).

Aim for at least 30 minutes of moderate-intensity exercise or physical activity per day, such as:

- **Brisk walking**

- **Jogging or running**

- **Swimming**

- **Cycling**

- **Yoga or Pilates**

- **Dancing**

- **Gardening or other outdoor activities**

Remember to listen to your body and start slowly, especially if you're new to exercise or have underlying health conditions. Consult with a healthcare professional before beginning any new exercise program.

CHAPTER 7:

TROUBLESHOOTING AND MAINTENANCE

COMMON CHALLENGES AND SOLUTIONS for troubleshooting and maintaining gut health:

Challenges:

1.**Constipation**: Infrequent bowel movements, hard stools, or difficulty passing stools.

2.**Bloating and Gas**: Feeling uncomfortably full or gassy.

3.**Abdominal Pain**: Cramping, sharp pains, or tenderness in the abdomen.

4. **Diarrhea**: Frequent, loose, or watery stools.

5. **Food Intolerances**: Adverse reactions to certain foods.

6. **Stress and Anxiety**: Emotional distress affecting gut health.

Solutions:

1. **Constipation**: Increase fiber intake, hydration, and physical activity. Consider probiotics or stool softeners.

2. **Bloating and Gas**: Eat smaller meals, avoid trigger foods, and try over-the-counter remedies like Beano or Gas-X.

3. **Abdominal Pain**: Identify and avoid trigger foods, manage stress, and consider anti-inflammatory supplements like turmeric or ginger.

4. **Diarrhea**: Stay hydrated, avoid irritants like caffeine or alcohol, and consider probiotics or anti-diarrheal medication.

5. **Food Intolerances**: Identify and avoid trigger foods, explore alternative options, and consult a healthcare professional.

6. **Stress and Anxiety:** Practice stress management techniques like meditation, yoga, or deep breathing exercises.

Additional Tips:

- **Listen to your body:** Pay attention to gut feelings and symptoms.

- **Seek professional help**: Consult a healthcare professional if challenges persist.

- **Stay hydrated**: Drink plenty of water throughout the day.

- **Get Enough sleep:** Aim for 7-8 hours of sleep per night.

- **Exercise regularly**: Engage in physical activity that brings you joy.

Remember, everyone's gut health journey is unique. Be patient, persistent, and kind to your gut!

MAINTAINING GUY HEALTH AND PREVENTING RELAPSE

Maintaining gut health and preventing relapse requires a long-term commitment to healthy habits and self-care.

Strategies to help you achieve this:

1. **Stick to a balanced diet:** Focus on whole, unprocessed foods, fruits, vegetables, whole grains, lean proteins, and healthy fats.

2. **Stay hydrated**: Drink plenty of water throughout the day.

3. **Exercise regularly:** Engage in physical activity that brings you joy, such as walking, yoga, or swimming.

4. **Manage stress**: Practice stress-reducing techniques like meditation, deep breathing, or journaling.

5. **Get enough sleep**: Aim for 7-8 hours of sleep per night.

6. **Monitor your symptoms**: Keep track of your gut

health and adjust your habits as needed.

7. **Avoid trigger foods**: Identify and avoid foods that can trigger gut issues.

8. **Consider probiotics:** Take probiotics regularly to support gut health.

9. **Stay connected**: Build a support network of friends, family, or a therapist.

10. **Be kind to yourself**: Practice self-compassion and prioritize your well-being.

Remember, maintaining gut health is a journey, and it's okay to encounter setbacks. By following these strategies and being patient and persistent, you can reduce the likelihood of relapse and enjoy long-term gut health and well-being.

CUTTING-EDGE METHODS FOR THE BEST POSSIBLE GUT HEALTH :

- **Eat more fruits and vegetables**: Try to include at least thirty different plant-based meals in your weekly diet.

- **Include nuts and seeds:** Include almonds, cashews, chia seeds, and pumpkin seeds in your diet, among others.1

- **Include legumes**: Consume prebiotic fiber-containing legumes, such as lentils, peas, and chickpeas.

- **Select whole grains:** Whole grains high in fiber include bulgur, quinoa, and oats.

- **Eat prebiotic foods**: Include in your diet whole wheat bread, onions, and bananas, among other foods high in prebiotics.

- **Eat fermented foods high in probiotics**: Indulge in foods high in probiotics, such as kefir, sauerkraut, and yogurt.

- **Drink coffee**: Studies indicate that coffee may encourage variety in the gut microbiota.

 Steer clear of highly processed foods: Restrict intake of refined carbohydrates, salt, and harmful fats.

- **Reduce sugar intake:** Cut less on sugar to support a healthy gut microbiota.

- Get enough sleep: To maintain gut health, aim for 7-8 hours of sleep every night.

Work out frequently: To encourage variety in the gut microbiota, partake in low-intensity exercises.

- **Practice stress management:** Look for techniques to de-stress, such as deep breathing exercises or meditation.

- **Avoid smoking**: Smoking has been related to detrimental impacts on health and a less diversified gut microbiome.

CONCLUSION

SUMMARY OF THE KEY TAKEAWAYS FOR TEA TREE OIL:

Uses:

- Acne treatment

- Athlete's foot treatment

- Dandruff and cradle cap treatment

- Head lice treatment

- Insect repellent

- Minor cut and abrasion treatment

- Nail fungus treatment

- Natural deodorant

- Oral health

Benefits:

- Antibacterial properties

- Anti-inflammatory properties

- Antifungal properties

- Antiviral properties

- Insecticidal properties

Safety and Precautions:

- Never swallow tea tree oil

- Do a patch test before using

- Dilute with a carrier oil for skin use

- Avoid using undiluted oil on skin

- Avoid using on children and pets

- Consult a healthcare professional before using

Additional Tips:

- Always choose a high-quality oil from a reputable source

- Follow proper dilution guidelines

- Use in moderation and as directed

- Be aware of potential allergic reactions

CONCLUDING REMARKS REGARDING THE PROSPECTS OF GUT HEALTH AND TEA TREE OIL RESEARCH:

Intestinal Health

- Current studies on the relationship between gut health and chronic illnesses including diabetes and heart disease; - Research on the gut-brain axis and its effects on mental health

A stronger emphasis on gut health and customized nutrition

Tea Tree Oil Studies

- Ongoing investigation on the antibacterial qualities and possible uses of tea tree oil

- Research on the antioxidant and anti-inflammatory

properties of tea tree oil

- Ongoing research on the potential benefits of tea tree oil for skincare and wound healing

Next Steps

Research on gut health and tea tree oil being incorporated into mainstream medicine; new goods and treatments that take use of these two factors are developed.

- Raising public and healthcare professional awareness and educating them

Potential Developments

The identification of novel strains of gut-healthy bacteria and the creation of tea tree oil-based remedies for a range of ailments

- Personalized medicine techniques that incorporate research on tea tree oil and gastrointestinal health

We can open up new avenues for enhancing human health and wellbeing by deepening our understanding of tea tree oil and gut health.